33023/17

MAKE YOUR OWN

CHESS SET

by David Carroll

Prentice-Hall, Inc., Englewood Cliffs, N.J.

Printed in the United States of America •J

Prentice-Hall International, Inc., London
Prentice-Hall of Australia, Pty. Ltd., North Sydney
Prentice-Hall of Canada, Ltd., Toronto
Prentice-Hall of India Private Ltd., New Delhi
Prentice-Hall of Japan, Inc., Tokyo

Library of Congress Cataloging in Publication
Data

Carroll, David, 1942—
    Make your own chess set.

    SUMMARY: Introduces the history of chess
and chess pieces and gives instructions for making twenty-five different chess sets out of easily
available materials.
    1. Chessmen—Juvenile literature. 2. Hand-
icraft—Juvenile literature. 3. Chess—History
—Juvenile literature.
    [1. Chessmen. 2. Handicraft] I. Title.
TT896.55.C37   731′.89′7941   74-8224
ISBN 0-13-547802-2

MAKE YOUR OWN
CHESS SET

INSTRUCTIONAL MATERIALS CENTER
GRISSOM MIDDLE SCHOOL
Mishawaka, Indiana

TABLE OF CONTENTS

THE OLDEST GAME

Chess is one of the oldest and most mysterious games known to man. It was played many centuries before Caesar marched through the streets of Rome, and to this day no one knows how or where it started. Was it, as legend tells, devised by Helen of Troy to divert the Greeks from their war against the Trojans? Or did a Chinese general learn of the game in a dream and use it to instruct his army in the arts of war and diplomacy? Was Good King Solomon or the Greek philosopher Aristotle really its inventor? No one knows.

Scholars now believe, however, that chess began in India. A game called *chaturanga* was played there for many centuries before the birth of Christ. Legend claims that this game, which in some ways resembles modern chess, was invented by a clever peasant to amuse a king. The king found this game immediately to his liking, and in gratitude offered the peasant, Sarsa, any reward he wished. "I am a humble man," replied Sarsa, "and require but a few coins with which to live out the last of my poor days. If Your Majesty would be so kind: on the first square of the game board place but a single gold coin; on the second square place but twice this number of coins, or two; on the third square place but twice this number again, or four; and so on, until all sixty-four squares are covered." The king could not quarrel with this seemingly modest request and set his ministers to the task. It was only later, when the ministers returned with mournful expressions and empty purses, that the ruler realized his mistake. If all the squares were filled in the manner requested by the humble Sarsa, exactly 18,446,744,973,709,551,661 gold coins would be needed —more money than has been minted since the beginning of recorded civilization.

At first glance the game of *chaturanga* seems similar to modern chess. The king sat on the same square he now does in chess. The castles and knights also occupied their familiar positions. The queen's square was filled, but by a piece known as the minister. And, as in today's game, the object of the contest was to capture the king. But here the likeness ends. Instead of bishops there were chariots, instead of pawns there were foot soldiers. The game required four players rather than two, and the pieces themselves could advance only one square at a time. Furthermore, the moves were not planned in advance, nor was it possible to develop a strategy. Everything was decided by the throw of dice, making *chaturanga* less a game of skill than one of blind chance.

This early version of chess remained the property of the Indians until the 6th century, when it migrated—scholars are not sure how and why—to neighboring Persia. The Persian poet Firdausi, in his poem the *Shahnama*, gives an account, probably legendary, of its introduction there. During the reign of Khosrau I Anushirvan (531–57), a contingent of Indian ambassadors arrived in Persia with a chessboard and pieces, announcing to the Persian ruler that unless he could discover the secrets of the game, he would be forced to pay tribute to the Indian monarchy. The king requested seven days grace and it was allowed. During this time he and his courtiers labored in vain to understand the principles of the game. Just as hope seemed lost, a servant who had been watching the whole affair stepped forward and offered his solution. It was correct; Persia was saved.

After its arrival in Persia this game, which now resembled chess more than *chaturanga*, spread through the world with astounding speed. In the early Middle Ages caravans loaded with travelers were a common sight on the Persia-to-Arabia highway, and from Arabia these journeyers traveled the highways of the earth. Chess traveled with them. Within a few centuries the game was played almost everywhere. In Mongolia, for instance, two kings went to war over the outcome of a contested chess match. In Baghdad chess was a favorite of the caliphs, and a Baghdadian poet, Abu Hafs, is said to have been the first man to play an opponent blindfolded. In Arabia historians tell us of enormous ivory chessmen which were used by the kings. During the games a man would stand by to carry the pieces from one square to another. In Russia, Burma, even far-off Borneo, the game of chess found a home. Indeed, it can rightly be said that from the 6th to the 10th century chess conquered the world.

During these years, probably sometime in the 10th century, chess arrived in Europe. It came to Spain via the Muslim invaders, to Italy via Byzantium, and to France and Scandinavia via returning Crusaders who learned the game from their Saracen enemy. As elsewhere, chess caught on immediately. Norman kings played it on the way to and from their battles, and one French king named his treasury department after the checkered chess board (hence the word *exchequer*, which in Britain is a title for the royal treasury). Almost all the rulers of medieval Europe enjoyed the sport, and it soon became known as the "game of kings." Yet, though the popes themselves occasionally indulged, chess was officially considered profane by the Church. "Was it right, I say," wrote St. Peter Damian to a certain bishop who had been caught amusing himself with chess, "and consistent with thy duty to sport away thy evenings amidst the vanity of chess, and defile the hand which offers up the body of the Lord . . . with the pollution of a sacrilegious game?"

Like other players before them, chess lovers in the West made their own contributions to the rules of chess. Alphonse of Castile, when he heard that an oriental emperor had replaced the knights with carved giraffes, was not to be outdone; he ordered two unicorns and a court jester added to his board along with the regular pieces. In Italy chessmen that were half knight, half rook were all the rage, along with queens that moved like knights and knights that moved like queens.

Out of all this, however, came the changes that led to modern chess. Castling, for instance, developed in medieval Europe. So did the checkered chessboard (originally all the squares were the same color). The bishop gained in the number of squares he could move at one time. The powers of the queen were vastly increased, and pawns were allowed to jump two squares upon opening. Gradually the modern game emerged and developed. By the 19th century, masters like Morphy, Capablanca, and Lasker were giving chess a heritage and were helped by the efforts of such men as Alexander Alekhine, who sometimes played twenty-nine games simultaneously without ever looking at the boards. Finally, in the 20th century, television and the news media so increased interest in the pastime that it is now the most popular indoor game in the world.

And so it will no doubt remain. The reason is clear: chess is so simple a child can learn the moves; yet it has such depth that the greatest geniuses of the chessboard cannot exhaust its possibilities. It is, in short, the most imaginative, the most unpredictable, and the most difficult intellectual puzzle ever devised by man.

CHESS SETS IN HISTORY

In this book are chess sets made of the most unlikely materials, such as nails, cookies, door latches, bathroom tiles, light switches, playing cards, and ball bearings. At first it may seem peculiar to consider sets made of such things, but it is all part of a time-honored tradition. Throughout history chess sets have been made of strange and unexpected materials.

In 16th century India Akbar the Great played an afternoon game of chess with real elephants and horses. Two generations later Akbar's grandson, Shah Jahan, used dancing girls as pieces and a whole garden for the board. Shah Jahan sat high in his marble tower calling each move from his throne and watched the beautiful living chess pieces whirl from square to square. Some years later, in Madras, India, visitors witnessed an equally remarkable sight—chessmen over twenty-five feet tall, mounted on wheeled platforms, were pulled across a colossal chessboard by teams of fifty men.

Of course not all chess sets have been so spectacular. The materials traditionally have been wood, metal, and ivory. These have been used for thousands of years, often with breath-taking results. One ancient Chinese set was crafted with each of its figures mounted on an ivory ball within which seven other ivory balls, each of decreasing size, turned freely one inside the other, a feat of carving which still remains unexplained.

In Europe the first known chess pieces date from the 13th century. They were carved from chunks of mottled ivory. Discovered in Scotland as part of the stock belonging to a ship-wrecked trader, they are called the Lewis Chessmen and almost seven complete sets of them exist today. Still in their original boxes when found, these wonderful little carvings had obviously been well cared for. This was only to be expected, for chess sets were highly valued during the Middle Ages. You can still see last wills and testaments which mention a father who left "that goode crystall set of myne" to his favorite son, or a rich merchant expressing a desire that his "ivorie chess warriors" be packed away with him in his tomb. It is also recorded that King Harold Hardraad of Norway in 1050 considered his three most precious possessions to be a white bear, a skull inlaid with gold, and a set of chessmen made of walrus teeth.

Medieval chess pieces, ordinarily quite large and of great weight, were at times used for more than just a friendly game. William the Conqueror is supposed to have hit a prince of France over the head with a chessboard. Charlemagne's son, upon losing a chess match to Okar the Bavarian, killed his poor opponent by clubbing him to death with an ivory rook!

There is still a long list of more unusual substances that have been enlisted by chess set makers throughout the centuries. Among these are glass, jade, papier-mache, gold, leather, sea shells, teeth, ebony, pewter, jewelry, wicker, bones, porcelain, mounted butterflies, cork, stainless steel, paper, rock crystal, silver, wax, lava, plaster of Paris, and clay. When none of these materials was available, the imagination of chess players did not fail. In 20th century Russian jails political prisoners make sets from bread crumbs and shreds of dried meat, while in Siberian labor camps captives fashion chess pieces from snow. During the Civil War soldiers created games from pebbles and twigs, and in World War I thirty-calibre cartridges made admirable pieces. Even today in New Guinea the natives play an unusual version of the game using stones as the major chessmen and dried insects as pawns.

Throughout the years chess sets have used a wider variety of materials, perhaps, than any other game. The character of the chess pieces allows for this variation. In fact, if you look around at nature and at man, it becomes apparent that practically *anything* can somehow be made into a chess set.

THE CHARACTER OF THE CHESS PIECES

When speaking of the "character" of the chess pieces it must be understood that each piece on the playing board is not just the materials from which it is fashioned. It is a symbol of a real human being or institution. If one looks at the chessmen from this standpoint—and it is difficult to make worthwhile sets without doing so—one realizes that, just like people, every chessman has its own strengths and weaknesses, its own limitations and peculiarities. The best way to show these different qualities is to vary the shape, size and weight of each piece to mirror its particular personality. Here are a few guidelines:

THE KING—The king is the most important member of the cast of chess characters, simply because if he's lost, the game goes with him. At the same time he is a highly limited creature, since he is only capable of moving one square at a time, hiding behind the other pieces or castling out of sight. Yet despite the king's weaknesses, he is still the *king*, and he is the object of the entire game. Therefore he is traditionally the tallest, straightest and most impressive piece on the board. Often he is marked with a sign of royalty such as a crown, scepter, or robe. In the Electronic Chess Set, for instance, a screw and nut on the king's head make a perfect crown.

THE QUEEN—The queen is the real power of the chessboard. She is the totally equipped soldier, capable of moving in any direction she chooses for as many squares as she likes. She is feared and respected by all the other pieces. She is a woman, and her sex can be indicated by the shape of the chess piece. The queen should be tall and dignified, a head taller than the other pieces but shorter than the king. Her shape should have grace and balance, or, if possible, some distinguishing mark to indicate her sex. For example, in the Electronic Set the wire on the queen's head suggests long, wavy hair.

THE BISHOP—Next to the queen stands the bishop, the sly diplomat of the chess board. He does not have the crushing power of the queen. He is not a muscle man. Instead, he approaches all matters of chess from angles, lying in wait on his diagonal square, preparing to glide across the board to snatch a sleeping opponent. The bishop stands a head shorter than the queen and slightly taller than the knight or castle. Think of him shaped as a long, narrow tube, the thinnest of the players. In some sets he wears a pointed or rounded cap to indicate his connection with the church. The hat worn by the bishop in the Electronic Chess Set is typical. In other sets the bishop's relationship with religion can be shown with a cross or other religious symbol. He stands for the power of the Church—just as the king represents the state, the knight the army, the castle commerce and trade, and the pawns the peasants.

THE KNIGHT—Half man, half horse, the knight is essential to chess strategy. While the bishop works on a sly slant, the knight jumps over his opponents and can be a devastating trap to his enemies. His fleet-footedness should be suggested by his stance. Although knight and bishop are equal in value, the knight is usually (but not always) slightly shorter than the bishop. And since the knight is half horse, part of his figure may be hooked or curved in imitation of a horse's neck. If it is not possible to make the knight *look* like a horse, his shape can *suggest* one. For instance, you can use a spring to construct part of his body, giving him a bouncy, ready-for-action air. In the Electronic Chess Set the lower body suggests the horse, and the thinness and tilt of the upper part suggest a rider.

THE CASTLE—On many chess sets the castle is shown as an elephant. Little wonder. The castle is a brute—as powerful as an elephant and just as determined. There is nothing subtle about him. He knows only straight lines, ahead or to the side. Yet he is considered of greater value than either the crafty bishop or the nimble knight. Indeed, if the bishop is an arrow and the knight a charging cavalryman, the castle is a Sherman tank. Weight rather than height is the key to making the castle. He should be heavy, ponderous, and broad, as in the Electronic Chess Set. He is what the name *castle* implies—a solid fortress.

THE PAWN—Last and truly least is the pawn. There is no democracy in chess. All men are created decidedly unequal, and pawns are the least equal of the lot. These humble slaves of the major pieces are like the serfs of an earlier age. Each is expected to sacrifice his life at any move for the good of a superior. But make no mistake. In the pawn beats a noble heart. He will never back down, even when threatened by a queen. Pawns should be the smallest pieces on the board, measuring no more than half the size of the bishop and a quarter the size of the king. All must look the same. Nothing about them must catch our attention—for if the pawns outshined the king, there is little doubt that the great monarch, in all his vanity, would deal with them severely.

MAKING THE SETS

Each section in this book features a unique chess set. The sets can be assembled from simple items that can be found in the kitchen, living room, or cellar. Most of the sets are extremely sturdy and are suitable for gifts or display. The only exceptions are the sets made of food, which you can (and sometimes must) eat when the game is over.

Each chapter has a list of materials required for making a complete chess set, both black and white pieces. The instructions for making the sets and the illustrations accompanying the instructions describe the procedure for *one side only*, sometimes black, sometimes white. Simply duplicate the same instructions for making the other side.

If you are not always able to find the materials we use in the demonstration sets, you can substitute materials you feel are acceptable. The important thing is the *concept* of the set, the *idea*, not the details of its construction. The methods recommended to make the sets are also not sacred. They are just guidelines to get you started on your own. The main purpose of this book is to encourage you to recognize creative materials *everywhere*, not just in the hobby shops or department stores, and to make chess sets that appeal to you. Manipulating simple materials in a way that expresses your ideas and individuality can be extremely relaxing and satisfying. Original chess sets also make great presents. They are inexpensive and highly personal.

METAL CHESS SETS

THE SCREW CHESS SET

Here is a set both interesting to look at and easy to construct. The pieces would make fitting opponents for the chessmen in the Nail Chess Set (page 23). Like the other hardware sets in this book, the materials can be purchased in any hardware store. And there are thousands of different types of screws you can choose from for variety.

WHAT YOU WILL NEED TO MAKE THE SET

2—1¾″ molly bolts
2—1½″ Phillips head
    metal screws
4—1¼″ round-head
    metal screws
4—1″ wood screws
4—¾″ round head
    brass screws

16—½″ wood screws
32—1″ x 1″ porcelain
    bathroom tiles, 16 white
    and 16 black (or
    colored)
felt (optional)
scissors
plastic cement

HOW TO MAKE THE SET:

THE BASES—The bases for this set are made of square 1″ (or 1½″ if you prefer) bathroom tiles, available at any hardware or plumbing supply store. Usually these tiles come in several colors. But if you can find only white ones, paint sixteen of them black and leave the others their natural color. If you do decide to paint the bases, be sure to paint them *before* you mount the pieces.

You can add a touch of elegance to the set by gluing patches of fitted felt to the bottom of each base. Felt also prevents the tiles from scratching the board. To do this use one of the tile bases as a cutting guide and cut out thirty-two squares. With plastic cement (or rubber cement if you plan to remove the patches in the future) glue these squares onto the bottom of the bases. Make certain the glue is spread over the entire surface of the patch, especially the corners and ends. Let the glue dry for at least six hours. Trim any overlap.

THE KING—Squeeze a large drop of clear plastic cement onto the center of a white tile. Set a 1¾″ molly bolt into the glue. Prop up the molly bolt with small blocks of wood or any other solid object while it's drying. Be sure the piece is straight as it sets. Once the glue is dry it's too late to make changes. Allow it to set overnight before using.

THE QUEEN—Using a 1½″ Phillips head metal screw, repeat the gluing and setting procedure used for the king. We used a Phillips head screw for the queen because the cross on the screwhead can be taken as a symbol of royalty. Any time such a sign occurs naturally on one of the materials, it can be put to use.

THE BISHOPS—Mount a 1¼″ round-head metal screw onto a white tile base, using the gluing and setting procedure described for the king. Let dry. Repeat this procedure for second bishop.

THE KNIGHTS—As always, the knight should be the slightly eccentric piece on the board, the maverick. Here we stand him upside down. Place a drop of glue onto a white tile. Set a 1″ wood screw into the glue headfirst and allow it to dry. Repeat this procedure for the second knight. The flat head of the wood screw will balance on its own and needs no props to support it while drying.

THE CASTLES—Glue and set a ¾″ round-head brass screw in the manner described for the king. Let dry. Repeat this procedure for second castle. By using brass screws, the castles are given the emphasis they deserve and the set is neatly balanced in overall design (you might think of the castles as heavy book ends hemming in all the other pieces and giving them support).

THE PAWNS—Glue and mount a ½″ wood screw upside down, as done with the knight. Let dry. Repeat this procedure for seven remaining pawns.

THE NAIL CHESS SET

This set makes use of the simple carpenter's nail. The materials can be purchased for pennies at any hardware store. The pieces can be embellished by painting parts of the nails—for instance, white on the head of the king nail to accentuate his crown, a broad stripe around the queen nail to indicate her robes, etc. Decorating the pieces can help you identify them while you're playing the game.

WHAT YOU WILL NEED TO MAKE THE SET

2—ten-penny brick nails
2—eight-penny common nails
4—flooring nails
4—underlayment nails
4—drywall nails
16—1½" finishing nails

5'—1" x 2" pine
T square, ruler and pencil
saw
fine sandpaper
black and white paint with brushes
hammer

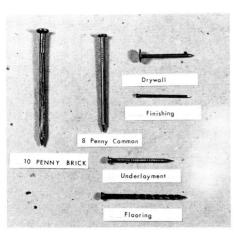

HOW TO MAKE THE SET:

THE BASES—The first step is to cut the bases on which the pieces will rest. Measure thirty-two 1½″ spaces along the five feet of 1″ x 2″ pine, using a ruler and pencil. Mark a line across the wood at each measurement point with your T square. Press the handle of the T square tight across the pine, as shown, to insure a perfect right angle. Saw through the wood along each line. Then go over the bases with fine sandpaper, smoothing the rough spots and raw edges. Paint sixteen of the bases black and sixteen of them white. (If you wish to stain the bases instead of painting them, see the stain chart on page 61.)

THE KING—Make a dot in the *exact* center of a wooden base. To find the center, cut a piece of paper 1½″ x 2″. Using a ruler, draw a diagonal line from corner to corner. The point where the two lines intersect is the exact center of the paper. Put your paper pattern over the base and stick the pencil through the paper and into the wood.

THE QUEEN—Center an eight-penny nail and tap it into a base.

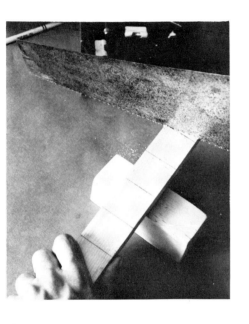

Note that the king and queen are both made of similarly shaped nails, but that the nail used for the queen is shorter and more slender.

THE BISHOPS—Mount a flooring nail, using the procedure described above. Repeat for second bishop.

THE KNIGHTS—Mount an underlayment nail, using the procedure described above. Repeat for second knight.

THE CASTLES—Mount a drywall nail using the procedure described above. Repeat for second castle.

THE PAWNS—Mount a 1½″ finishing nail, using the procedure described above. Repeat for seven remaining pawns.

> *NOTE:* Be sure all the nails are standing perfectly straight in their bases or the effect of the set will be ruined. If any are tilted, a light tap with a hammer (or even the fingers) on the appropriate side should push them upright.

THE BALL BEARING CHESS SET

Ball bearings are small stainless steel or brass balls used to reduce friction in the moving parts of a machine. Here we will borrow these tools of technology and put them on the chess table. This set requires no cutting, sawing or measuring. The only time-consuming element is finding the parts themselves. Ball bearings can usually be purchased at a hardware store. If you can't find them there, try an automobile repair shop or a machine shop.

WHAT YOU WILL NEED TO MAKE THE SET

4—1" stainless steel ball
    bearings
2—¹⁄₁₆" ball bearings
4—½" brass ball bearings
4—⅝" stainless steel ball
    bearings
4—¼" stainless steel ball
    bearings

20—³⁄₁₆" ball bearings
16—flat 1½" gear plates
    with ½" hole in center
16—tee-nut fasteners
    for metal
black and white metal
    paint with brushes
glue

1"   1"⁄2   5"⁄8

Tee-nut Fastener

1"⁄4   3"⁄16   1"⁄16

Gear Plate

HOW TO MAKE THE SET:

THE BASES—Paint eight gear plates and eight tee-nut fasteners white (and the same number black for the opposite side). Place them on a clean surface and allow to dry.

THE KING—Place a tiny drop of glue directly on the top of a 1″ ball bearing. Let this drop set for thirty seconds and place a ¹⁄₁₆″ ball bearing into it. Hold till the ¹⁄₁₆″ ball bearing no longer wobbles. Run a little glue around the center rim of a black flat gear plate. Place the 1″ ball bearing into it, making sure the ¹⁄₁₆″ ball bearing is sticking straight up. This is the king's crown and serves to distinguish him from the queen. Wipe off the excess glue and let dry.

THE QUEEN—Run glue around the inside rim of another black flat gear plate. Place a 1″ ball bearing on top and let dry.

THE BISHOPS—Glue a ½″ brass ball bearing onto a black gear plate and let dry. Repeat for second black bishop. Brass adds variety of appearance to this set, which might otherwise look a trifle monotonous.

28

THE KNIGHTS—Glue a ¼″ ball bearing into a black gear plate base, and let dry. Squeeze a drop of glue on top of the ¼″ ball bearing and let it set for thirty seconds. Place a ³⁄₁₆″ ball bearing onto it, holding it there until the ³⁄₁₆″ ball bearing no longer wobbles. Let dry. Repeat this procedure for second knight.

THE CASTLES—Glue a ⅝″ ball bearing onto a black gear plate base. Let dry. Repeat for second castle.

THE PAWNS—Run a line of glue around the top rim of a black tee-nut fastener. Place a ³⁄₁₆″ ball bearing on this top rim and let dry. Repeat for seven remaining pawns.

> *NOTE:* Stainless steel looks best when polished. Buff this set with metal polish and a soft rag.

THE PLUMBING PARTS CHESS SET

The least attractive objects sometimes make the most handsome chess pieces. Take, for example, household plumbing fixtures—not exactly the items usually found in a craftsman's studio, let alone in a living room. Yet if you take certain of these fixtures—elbows, nuts and couplings—and combine them in a thoughtful way, many interesting results will follow. Most of the materials for this set are found on the racks of plumbing supply houses. If such a store does not exist in your vicinity, many hardware shops stock plumbing parts. You might also try the handyman sections of the larger department stores.

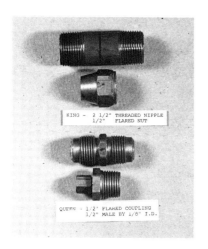

KING – 2 1/2" THREADED NIPPLE
1/2" FLARED NUT

QUEEN – 1/2" FLARED COUPLING
1/2" MALE BY 1/8" I.D.

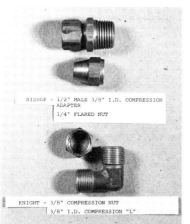

BISHOP – 1/2" MALE 3/8" I.D. COMPRESSION
ADAPTER
1/4" FLARED NUT

KNIGHT – 3/8" COMPRESSION NUT
3/8" I.D. COMPRESSION "L"

WHAT YOU WILL NEED TO MAKE THE SET

NOTE: The following list of materials is quite technical and no doubt almost indecipherable to the non-plumber. However, if you present it to a plumbing supply dealer, he will have no difficulty filling your order.

2—2½" threaded nipples
6—½" flared nuts
2—½" flared couplings
2—½" male by ⅛" I.D.
4—½" male ⅜" I.D. compression adapters
4—¼" flared nuts
4—⅜" compression nuts
4—⅜" I.D. compression "L"s

4—⅜" I.D. compression nuts
4—½" I.D. flared nuts
16—⅜" female by ⅛" compression adapters
32—1" porcelain bathroom tiles (four- or six-sided)
paint and brush
glue

HOW TO MAKE THE SET:

THE BASES—White one-inch porcelain bathroom tiles can be purchased at hardware or plumbing supply stores, and come either in square or six-sided shapes (we have used the six-sided variety). Paint sixteen of these bases black and leave sixteen of them their natural color for the opposing side. (*Do not* try to paint the bases once the brass fittings have been mounted onto them.) When the paint dries, assemble each piece by gluing it onto the base.

THE KING—Glue a 2½″ threaded nipple onto the center of a white base. Let dry. Place a thin coat of glue onto the top rim of the threaded nipple. Put the bottom of a ½″ flared nut on top of the nipple rim. Make sure that the rims of the nut and the nipple are perfectly aligned without any overlap. Allow to dry for twenty-four hours.

THE QUEEN—Glue a ½″ flared coupling to the center of a white base. Let dry. Place a small amount of glue onto the top rim of the ½″ flared coupling. Put the bottom of a ½″ male by ⅛″ I.D. into this glued rim. Let dry.

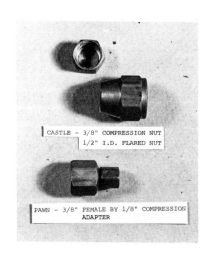

CASTLE - 3/8" COMPRESSION NUT
1/2" I.D. FLARED NUT

PAWN - 3/8" FEMALE BY 1/8" COMPRESSION ADAPTER

THE BISHOPS—Glue a ½″ male ⅜″ I.D. compression adapter to the center of a white base. Let dry. Place a small amount of glue into the top rim of the compression adapter. Put the bottom of the ¼″ flared nut into the glued rim. Let dry. Repeat this procedure for second bishop.

THE KNIGHTS—Glue a ⅜″ compression nut onto the center of a white base. Let dry. Screw a ⅜″ I.D. compression "L" into the ⅜″ compression nut. If you wish, you can squeeze a little glue on the thread of the nut before screwing it into the "L", to insure that the pieces will not come unscrewed. Repeat this procedure for second knight.

THE CASTLES—Glue a ⅜″ I.D. compression nut onto the center of a white base. Let dry. Place a small amount of glue on the rim of the compression nut. Place the narrowest part of a ½″ flared nut onto the glued rim. Let dry. Repeat this procedure for second castle.

THE PAWNS—Glue a ⅜″ female by ⅛″ compression adapter onto the center of a white base. No additional construction is required. Let dry. Repeat for seven remaining pawns.

> *NOTE:* When all the pieces are assembled and glued, let them stand overnight. Scrape off the excess glue that may have accumulated at the joints. An extra touch can be added by mounting pieces of felt onto the bottom of the bases. Instructions for the cutting and mounting of felt are given on page 20. Like ball bearings, plumbing fixtures look best when given a good polish with a rag and metal polish.

THE HOOK AND EYE CHESS SET

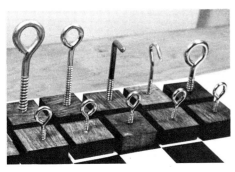

This set uses two common hardware items—metal hooks and eyes. Ordinarily these materials are screwed into a wall or ceiling in order to hang things like flowerpots or lamps. They are also used together as a door latch. But now they are partners in the name of chess. The set is easy to assemble and all materials can be found in any good dime or hardware store.

WHAT YOU WILL NEED TO MAKE THE SET

2—4″ metal screw eyes
2—3½″ metal screw eyes
4—3″ right angle screw
   hooks
4—2¼″ metal screw
   hooks

4—2½″ metal screw eyes
16—1½″ metal screw eyes
1—ten-penny nail
painted wooden bases
hammer

2½″ Eye   3½″ Eye   4″ Eye   3″ Angle Hook

2½″ Hook   1½″ Eye

HOW TO MAKE THE SET:

THE BASES—Use regular wooden bases for the Hook and Eye Chess Set. The instructions for these are given on page 24.

THE KING—Screw a 4″ metal screw eye into a wooden base. The screw thread on the larger hooks and eyes may be difficult to drive directly into the wood. To make things easier, tap a hole approximately ⅛″ deep in the center of the base with a hammer and a ten-penny nail. Place the 4″ metal screw eye into the hole and turn it several times until the screw thread bites into the wood and holds without wobbling. Do not force the screw into the hole. If the base shows any signs of cracking, stop and remove the screw. Widen the nail hole and try again.

THE QUEEN—Tap a hole in a base with a ten-penny nail, and screw in a 3½″ metal screw eye. Be sure it is mounted exactly in the middle of the base. This set will be seen from a number of different angles, and if a single piece is not centered, it will throw off the appearance of the whole set.

THE BISHOPS—Tap a hole in the center of a base with a ten-penny nail and screw in the 3″ right angle screw hook. Repeat for second bishop.

THE KNIGHTS—Tap a hole in the center of a base with a ten-penny nail and screw in a 2 ¼″ metal screw hook. Repeat for second knight.

THE CASTLES—Tap a hole in the center of a base with a ten-penny nail and screw in a 2 ½″ metal screw eye. Repeat for second castle.

THE PAWNS—Tap a hole in the center of a base with a ten-penny nail and screw in a 1 ½″ metal screw eye. Repeat for seven remaining pawns.

THE LAG BOLT CHESS SET

Lag bolts are ordinarily used to fasten and bolt heavy construction materials; yet these sturdy, beautifully engineered objects fit perfectly on the game board. Lag bolts can be found in most hardware stores. They are usually on display in large bins or on shelves. The next time you are in a hardware store, you might want to exercise your imagination by picturing the way household objects might be combined to make chessmen.

WHAT YOU WILL NEED TO MAKE THE SET

2—¾″ x 3½″ lag bolts	16—½″ washers
2—⅝″ x 3½″ lag bolts	black metallic paint
4—½″ x 3″ lag bolts	felt (optional)
8—½″ x 2″ lag bolts	scissors
4—½″ nuts	glue
16—½″ x 1½″ lag bolts	

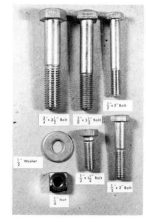

HOW TO MAKE THE SET:

THE BASES—The major pieces are glued onto ½″ washers, while the pawns stand on their own without support. Paint eight ½″ washers black (leave the same number their natural color for the white bases). If desired, felt pieces can be cut to size for each of the bases and attached to the bases with glue. (See page 20.)

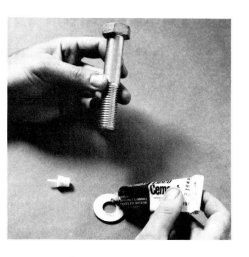

THE KING—Glue a ¾″ x 3½″ lag bolt head-down (upside down, as shown) onto a plain-colored washer base. In our set we have not decorated the king. However, a small ball bearing would make an interesting crown.

THE QUEEN—Glue a ⅝″ x 3½″ lag bolt head-up onto a plain-colored washer base, as shown. As with the king, a small object on top of the queen makes an effective mark for singling out the royal pieces. If the queen is given a headpiece, however, make certain it is not as large or as elaborate as that which crowns the king.

THE BISHOPS—Glue a ½" x 3" lag bolt head-down onto a plain-colored washer base. Let dry. Repeat this procedure for second bishop.

THE KNIGHTS—Glue a ½" x 2" lag bolt head-up onto a plain-colored washer base. Let dry. Repeat this procedure for second knight.

THE CASTLES—Glue a ½" x 2" lag bolt head-down onto a plain-colored washer base. Screw a ½" nut several turns onto the exposed thread projecting from the bolt. Let dry. Repeat this procedure for second castle.

THE PAWNS—Stand a ½" x 1½" lag bolt on the pawn's spot without a base. Repeat for seven remaining pawns.

> *NOTE:* This set can be arranged in a number of ways—the arrangement shown here is only one of them. Another set, quite different in style and feeling, can be produced with several minor changes. Try, for example, arranging all the pieces head-downward, as shown here. Or try staggering the pieces, one head-up, one head-down.

THE HOSE FIXTURE
CHESS SET

The Hose Fixture Chess Set is one of the most striking combinations presented in this book. It is also one of the most expensive to assemble. It is made completely of hose parts—nozzles, connecting joints and couplings. These pieces are composed almost totally of brass, and the price of brass is high. (The demonstration set shown here cost approximately $15.00—one side only.) You can try to economize by shopping at discount hardware stores. Or you can buy the parts directly from the manufacturer at wholesale prices, if possible. The parts for this set are usually stocked by hardware stores only in the summer months, when hose equipment is in demand. During the fall these materials sometimes go on sale, and then it is possible to pick them up for half the regular price.

WHAT YOU WILL NEED TO MAKE THE SET

2—male ¾" brass clinching hose couplings

2—female ¾" brass clinching hose couplings

8—male ⅝" brass clinching hose couplings

2—male ½" brass clinching hose couplings

2—female ½" brass clinching hose couplings

4—brass hose nozzles

4—brass standard-sized quick hose couplers

32—⅜" brass compression nuts

painted wooden bases

plastic cement

5/8" CLINCHING HOSE COUPLING

1/2" MALE CLINCHING COUPLING

1/2" FEMALE CLINCHING COUPLING

1/4" MALE CLINCHING COUPLING

3/4" FEMALE CLINCHING COUPLING

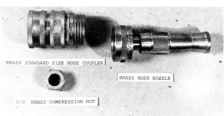

BRASS STANDARD SIZE HOSE COUPLER

BRASS HOSE NOZZLE

3/8" BRASS COMPRESSION NUT

HOW TO MAKE THE SET:

THE BASES—The Hose Fixture Chess Set requires regular wooden bases. The instructions for these are given on page 24.

THE KING—Screw a male ¾″ brass clinching hose coupling into a ¾″ female brass clinching hose coupling so that the pieces fit together tightly. If you wish to make this union permanent, add a little glue to the thread of the male clinching before joining. Cover one end of this male-female assembly with a thin coat of glue. Fit the male (threaded) end of a male ⅝″ brass clinching over the glued end, as shown. This clinching may jiggle slightly when you first put it on, but the glue should hold it fast within a few minutes. Let dry, then mount onto a wooden base with a little glue.

THE QUEEN—Screw a male ½″ brass clinching hose coupling into a ½″ female brass clinching hose coupling so that the pieces are tightly seated. If you wish to make this union permanent, add a little glue to the thread of the male coupling before joining. Cover one end of this male-female assembly with a thin coat of glue. Place this glued end into the unthreaded end of a male ⅝″

brass clinching hose coupling, as shown, so that the threaded end serves as base. Let dry, and mount onto the wooden base with a little glue.

THE BISHOPS—Place a little glue around the bottom rim of a brass hose nozzle and mount onto a wooden base. Repeat this procedure for second bishop.

THE KNIGHTS—Place a few drops of glue on the threaded end of a male ⅝″ brass clinching hose coupling. Mount this coupling onto its wooden base so that it lies on its side, in the picture of the demonstration set. Repeat this procedure for second knight.

THE CASTLES—Place a little glue onto the wider of the two nozzle ends of a brass standard-sized quick hose coupler. Mount it onto a wooden base, smaller end up, in the picture of the demonstration set. Repeat this procedure for second castle.

THE PAWNS—Place a bead of glue along one rim of a ⅜″ brass compression nut and mount it onto the center of a wooden base. Add a similar bead of glue to the rim of a second ⅜″ brass compression nut and mount it onto the first nut, making sure the edges are neatly aligned. Repeat this procedure for seven remaining pawns.

> *NOTE:* If you wish to make this set even more elaborate, several variations are possible. For example, the knight can be doubled in size by gluing a ⅝″ brass clinching coupling onto the first coupling, here. The castle can similarly be enlarged and beautified by crowning it with a ⅝″ brass clinching coupling, as shown in this same picture. Experiment on your own with other combinations.

TWO TECHNOLOGICAL CHESS SETS

THE ELECTRONIC CHESS SET

For many years artists have realized that the products of industry and technology make wonderful materials for sculpture and design. The electrical world contributes switches, fuses, plugs and sockets for an excellent chess set that requires no construction. The materials for this set can be located in any good hardware store and are not expensive.

WHAT YOU WILL NEED TO MAKE THE SET

2—4″ appliance plugs
2—3″ female sockets
4—45 amp fuses
4—socket lamp switches
4—1½″ twist-lock female sockets

16—female screw-in plugs
1—small can of white paint
1—½″ brush

HOW TO MAKE THE SET:

THE BASES—These electrical parts stand on their own. To identify the sides, paint the non-metallic parts of one side white.

THE KING—Place a 4″ appliance plug on the king's square, spring side up.

THE QUEEN—Place a 3″ female socket on the queen's square, using the widest part for the base.

THE BISHOPS—Place the 45 amp fuses on the bishops' squares.

THE KNIGHTS—Place the socket lamp switches, metallic side down, on the knights' squares.

THE CASTLES—Place the 1½″ twist-lock female sockets, metallic side up, on the castles' squares.

THE PAWNS—Place the female screw-in plugs, metallic side up, on the pawns' squares.

THE COMPONENTS CHESS SET

This set is made of electronic components which can be bought in electronics supply stores or in radio and television shops. Don't be distressed if you can't find the exact parts that are pictured here. There are literally a hundred thousand varieties of these parts manufactured each year, and no one outlet is likely to carry all of them. So if you run into trouble, substitute freely. The methods of construction described below are simple and can be adapted to your selections.

WHAT YOU WILL NEED TO MAKE THE SET

2—double-pole double-throws

2—lighted push-button switches

4—3″ television tubes

4—toggle switches

4—indicator light assemblies

16—resistors

painted wooden bases

glue

round or flat-nosed pliers

small finishing nail

HOW TO MAKE THE SET:

THE BASES—For instructions to make and paint wooden bases see page 24.

THE KING—Glue a double-pole double-throw onto a wooden base. Make sure the piece is standing in the center of the base. Let it dry overnight.

THE QUEEN—Glue a lighted push-button switch onto the center of a wooden base and let it dry overnight.

THE BISHOPS—Glue two 3″ television tubes onto wooden bases. Make sure each tube is placed in the center of its base. Let dry overnight.

THE KNIGHTS—Glue two toggle switches onto wooden bases and let them dry overnight.

THE CASTLES—Glue the indicator light assemblies onto wooden bases and let them dry overnight.

THE PAWNS—With a wire cutter snip off the wire on one end of a resistor. Leave the wire on the other end intact. Tap a hole in the center of a wooden base with a small finishing nail. Place a drop of glue into the hole and let it set for a minute. Put the wire end of the resistor into the hole and let it dry overnight. Repeat this process for the remaining pawns.

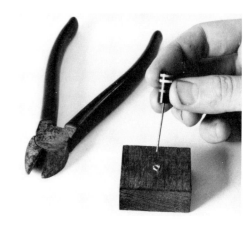

WOODEN CHESS SETS

THE BASIC WOODEN CHESS SET

Wood is an excellent material for making chess sets. It's light. It takes color and stain. It comes in many handsome varieties. It's cheap. And best of all, it lasts. The following instructions are for the basic set. The variations on this set are infinite; three decorative possibilities are included here.

WHAT YOU WILL NEED TO MAKE THE SET

1'—of 2" x 2" pine	pencil, ruler and T square
1'—1½" dowel	a saw, preferably a back-
4'—⅞" dowel	saw
18"—1" x 1" pine	plastic cement
1'—1¼" dowel	medium and fine sandpaper
6"—⅜" dowel	black and white paint (or stain)

HOW TO MAKE THE SET:

THE BASES—Each piece in the Wooden Chess Set balances on its own and requires no extra base to support it.

THE KING—On the 2″ x 2″ pine board, measure and mark off a 5″ length with a ruler and pencil. Pressing the T-square firmly against the side of the board, draw a line across the wood at the measurement point (see page 24 for an illustration of this procedure). Saw off the 5″ piece. Keep the saw exactly on the line and make slow, steady strokes. The back-saw is the best tool for making even cuts because of its small teeth and hard steel. Be sure that all cuts are straight. If they aren't, the bottom of the piece will be uneven and the pieces will wobble when you're trying to play.

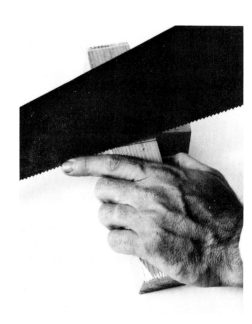

THE QUEEN—Saw off a 4½″ piece from the 1½″ dowel. Again make certain that the piece is cut evenly. Place on chess board as is.

THE BISHOPS—Saw off a 3¾″ piece from the ⅞″ dowel. If you wish to bevel the top of the bishop, as in the demonstration set, mark a diagonal line on the dowel with a pencil and gently saw this line. Short, steady strokes will keep the dowel from wobbling while you saw. If you still have difficulty, put the dowel in a vice or under clamps. Repeat this procedure for second bishop.

THE KNIGHTS—Cut a piece 3½″ in length from the 1″ x 1″ pine. Cut a ½″ piece from the ⅜″ dowel. Glue the piece of dowel onto the 3½″ pine at a point 3″ up from the bottom. (This nub represents the head of the knight's horse.) Let dry. Repeat this procedure for second knight.

THE CASTLES—Cut a piece 3″ in length from the 1¼″ dowel. Place on board as is. Repeat this procedure for second castle.

THE PAWNS—Cut a piece 2″ in length from the ⅞″ dowel (the same dowel from which the bishop was made). Place on board. Repeat for seven remaining pawns.

FINISHING OFF THE SET—The set is now ready to be sanded. With some medium grain sandpaper, clean off the rough edges and burrs left from the cutting. Go over each piece thoroughly with fine sandpaper, smoothing out all imperfections until the surfaces are smooth to the touch. Careful sanding is one of the most important steps in turning out a finished-looking chess set. You may now either paint the sets black and white or stain them with a dark and light stain. Stain serves two purposes. It gives rich color to the wood, and it preserves it. For the black side we'd suggest a deep, mellow stain like cherry or walnut. For the white side a pine stain is attractive. In the demonstration set a clear stain is used. Apply the stain with an old rag or paint brush. Use it sparingly, trying to bring out the natural grain of the wood as you brush it on. Two thin coats are best. Give each coat six hours to dry. When the second coat is finished, you can wax or varnish the set for further protection.

A GUIDE TO THE MOST POPULAR STAINS

clear—brings out the highlights of the wood rather than staining it.

pine—light reddish yellow

fruitwood—still very light but a little darker and more mellow than pine

oak—light golden brown

cherry—rich reddish brown middle tone

maple—light reddish brown

mahogany—very deep reddish brown

dark walnut—deep rich chocolate brown

ebony—black

THE WOODEN MONOGRAM CHESS SET

WHAT YOU WILL NEED TO MAKE THE SET

completed Wooden Chess Set

T square

pencil and ruler

brush and paints (or yellow and black magic markers)

HOW TO MAKE THE SET:

Before you monogram the pieces, it is a good idea to mark guidelines for your letters. On the king and queen, mark off a point two inches from the bottom of each piece, using a ruler and pencil. Mark off a second point 1½″ up from the first point. Use a T square to draw parallel lines across the pieces at the marked-off points.

Draw the initial of each piece, *K* for the king, *Q* for the queen, *B* for the bishop, etc. In the demonstration set, the letters are drawn free hand. Some people prefer to use a letter stencil, which can be found at most dime or stationery stores. Do not bear down too hard with the pencil while drawing in the letters or it will dig into the wood.

After the letters are sketched in pencil, carefully color in each of them, using a light color for the letters on the black side and a dark color for the letters on the white.

Here we have used water colors because they blend with the grain of the wood. However, oil paints, acrylics or magic markers do just as well. Let the paint dry for half a day. Erase the guidelines and the set is complete.

THE PAINTED WOODEN CHESS SET

WHAT YOU WILL NEED TO MAKE THE SET

completed Wooden Chess
   Set
pencil

brushes and paints (or
   colored magic markers)

64

HOW TO MAKE THE SET:

For this set, draw pictures of the chessmen onto the pieces themselves. You can invent your own portraits, as we have done in the demonstration set, or you can copy them from other pictures. They can be portraits of real people. For instance, you might design a set based on the royal family of England. You might draw one completely founded on a fantasy, such as a Chinese court with the emperor as king, empress as queen, ministers as bishops, warriors as knights, pagodas as castles and peasants as pawns. Cartoons, brief sketches with a pen, a few well-placed lines and circles, all can be effective. Whatever you do, the best way to proceed is to make a pencil sketch of each figure on a piece of paper *before* drawing it onto the chessman. Then copy it onto the chessman. Do *not* paint any of the pieces until you are sure of the design. Once paint goes onto wood it is practically impossible to remove.

A FEW MORE IDEAS

The Wooden Chess Set can be transformed into as many sets as there are people to create them. These few ideas seem worthy of exploration:

1—Paint the pieces with abstract designs—zigzag lines, blotches, spots, streaks, squares. Try making a set with one side polka dots and the other side stripes.

2—Paint each side with dayglow colors and play the game in the dark.

3—Paint one side gold and the other side silver.

4—Paint floral designs on the pieces—scrolls, loops, swirls, leaves, vines. Do a set of different flowers, i.e., the roses versus the carnations. The same might be done with trees, plants, etc.

5—Paint scenes on the chessmen: the landscapes versus the still lifes; or the countryscape versus the cityscape.

6—Paint silhouettes—of people, buildings, landscapes, etc.

7—Instead of using initial letters, as in the Wooden Monogram Set, write the entire name of each piece across the chessman in fine script. Or make up names; or use foreign names; or write numerals.

8—Draw animals rather than people: a lion and a lioness as king and queen, a hippopotamus as castle, monkeys as pawns, giraffes as bishops, zebras as knights, and so forth.

9—Paint the wooden pieces with a coat of rubber cement and cover them with sequins, glitter, jewelry findings, pebbles, or scraps of fabric. Try combining this effect with drawings between the glued-on scraps.

THE CONTAINER CHESS SET

This set shows what can be done with any nicely shaped box or container. We used unpainted wooden cartridge boxes designed to hold hunting shells. They were purchased at an army-navy surplus store. Similar items can be bought from any manufacturer of wooden containers. The boxes in this set are for demonstration purposes. They show what can be done with containers in general. Plastic containers can be used instead of wooden boxes. Or you might make a set from small bottles, empty cans, even milk cartons. Although the demonstration set here is left unfinished, it could have been painted, stained, ornamented with drawings, decals or collage: any of the methods presented in the Wooden Chess Set.

WHAT YOU WILL NEED TO MAKE THE SET

4—1″ wooden box tops
6—1¼″ wooden box tops
16—4″ x 1½″ wooden
   boxes
4—1⅔″ wooden box tops

16—2½″ x 1″ wooden
   boxes
glue
decorating materials as
   mentioned

HOW TO MAKE THE SET:

THE BASES—This set requires no bases. The black side can be distinguished from the white by coloring one side a dark color and the other side a light color. Bases, however, can be used if desired. The standard wooden bases described on page 24 will do the job. If a surplus of 1¾″ box tops is available, these can also be used. The plastic disc bases described in the Plastic Cube Chess Set also go well with the wooden containers.

THE KING—Glue a 1″ box top to the center of a 1¼″ box top. Let dry. Mount the joined tops onto the center of a 4″ wooden box. Let dry.

THE QUEEN—Remove the top of a 4″ wooden box, turn it upside down, and place it directly over the rim of this same box. Glue and let dry. Glue a 1″ wooden box top in the center of the reversed lid. Let dry.

THE BISHOPS—A 4″ by 1½″ wooden box serves as the bishop. Nothing need be done to it. Simply stand it on its square and repeat the procedure for the second bishop.

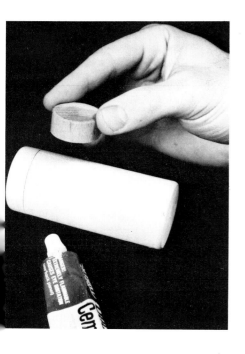

THE KNIGHTS—Glue a 1¼″ box top approximately an inch down from the top of a 4″ wooden box, as shown. As usual, such a protrusion indicates a horse's head and thus identifies the knight. Let dry. Repeat this procedure for the second knight, making sure that you glue the 1¼″ top at exactly the same height as the first.

THE CASTLES—Remove the top from a 4″ wooden box. Replace it with a 1⅔″ top, the type which fits the standard 4″ box. This extra-large top gives the necessary size and importance to the castle. Repeat this procedure for second castle.

THE PAWNS—A 2½″ by 1″ wooden box serves as the pawn. Nothing need be done to it. Simply stand it on its square, and repeat for seven remaining pawns.

PAPER CHESS SETS

74

THE PLAYING CARD CHESS SET

Some experts say that playing cards are an off-shoot of chess and that cards were invented during the Middle Ages to entertain a mad French king whose passion for chess had cooled. Whether or not this is true, there certainly are similarities between the two games. The king and queen are present in both. The pawns of chess correspond to the lesser cards in the deck, from the ten to the deuce. The knight of chess seems a good deal like the joker. And in European decks, there is even an opposite number for the bishop —the page. With such obvious likenesses, it is not a trick to turn a deck of cards into a "deck" of chess.

WHAT YOU WILL NEED TO MAKE THE SET

painted wooden bases   four decks of playing cards
pencil, ruler, T square   scissors
a fine-toothed saw   rubber cement

HOW TO MAKE THE SET:

THE BASES—For the Playing Card Chess Set we will use the regular wooden bases. Instructions for these are given on page 24. After you have prepared the bases, draw a pencil line down the exact center of each base. Make a cut approximately ⅛″ deep along each line with a fine-toothed saw. (The smaller the teeth of your saw, the finer the cut will be.) Saw with short, light strokes to help keep your bases from wiggling while you're making the cut. If you still have trouble, put the bases in a vice or C-clamp while you saw them. The cut in each base should be deep enough so that a card will sit in it comfortably.

THE PIECES—Pull out the kings, queens, jacks, tens, and jokers from all four decks of cards. Set the rest of the cards aside. Sort the honor cards into two piles, one red and one black. The red will represent the white chessmen, and the black will represent the black side.

THE KING—Take two king of hearts from the red pile. Notice the figures of the kings are enclosed in white rectangles. Cut out the figures of the kings with scissors, using this white rectangle as your outside cutting guide. If you crop properly there should now be two diamond kings exactly the same size. Cover the *back* of each king with rubber cement and press the two backs together. Wipe any excess cement off the edges and place the piece on a clean piece of paper to dry.

THE QUEEN—Follow the directions for the king, using two diamond queens.

THE BISHOPS—Take two diamond tens and two heart tens from your pile of honor cards. Cut the king figure out of the white rectangle of a left-over red king. This will be your cutting guide. Place the cutting guide in the exact center of a ten, covering the spots completely. In pencil, lightly draw an outline around the cutting guide. Trim along this pencil-line border. When all the tens have been cut in this way, paste two of them back-to-back, suit-to-suit (the diamonds together and hearts together) with rubber cement. Do the same thing with the remaining two tens.

78

THE KNIGHTS—Follow the cutting directions for the bishops, using four jokers or four aces.

THE CASTLES—Take two diamond jacks and two heart jacks from your pile of honor cards. Using your king cutting guide, trim the jacks within their rectangles the same way you did for the king and the queen. Paste two of them back-to-back, suit-to-suit with rubber cement. Do the same for the second castle.

THE PAWNS—The pawns are made of single hearts and diamonds, each measuring one-quarter of the size of the whole card. (Make your pawns from the ace, two, three, or four cards. Cards numbered five and up have too many pips on them to be useful.) Using a ruler as a guide, draw a square around a single diamond. Cut it out. It will serve as your cutting guide for the remaining pawns. Cut out eight single hearts and eight single diamonds. Paste the diamonds back-to-back in pairs. Do the same for the hearts.

ASSEMBLING THE SET—Place a drop of rubber cement into the cut on a wooden base. When the rubber cement has nearly dried, set your king into the cut. Allow to dry for an hour. Repeat this process for the remaining pieces.

Use the spades and clubs you have set aside to make the black pieces for your set.

THE PAPER CUTOUT SET

If you have ever spent time cutting out patterns, collages, cameos, etc., this set will be a simple one for you to make. It consists of cut out silhouettes of the chessmen. The set can be as artistic as you care to make it. Elaborate silhouettes can be cut, or the pieces can be scissored into simple block-like shapes. The demonstration set presented here is somewhere in the middle, neither painstakingly intricate nor overly crude. Try making a version of this set first; then, once you have a feeling for it, go on to make whatever style you wish. Some suggestions are given at the end of the chapter for further ideas.

WHAT YOU WILL NEED TO MAKE THE SET

stiff, heavy paper—½ light-colored, ½ dark (six 9″ x 12″ sheets or equivalent amount)

ruler	*pencil and eraser*
scissors	*paper-hole puncher*

NOTE: white file cards may be used instead of white construction paper. These were used in the demonstration set.

HOW TO MAKE THE SET:

THE BASES—(See directions for size, cutting etc. of the pieces before referring to this section on bases.)

Make a straight crease approximately ¾″ from the bottom of each piece. Fold back and forth along the crease several times, then fold the bottom flap under as shown, so that this tab acts as a support. This fold must be straight; otherwise the piece will not stand properly erect. To insure a straight fold, mark the fold line with a pencil before turning it under, so that you know exactly where to fold. Or you can make the actual crease over the edge of a ruler or any straight-edged implement, so that the fold line is evenly marked.

THE KING—Cut a strip 4½″ long by 1½″ wide from a piece of white construction paper. Using your pencil, sketch the lines of the king's crown on one end of the strip. When the crown is drawn to your satisfaction, use scissors to cut carefully along these lines. Crease the bottom of the figure to make the base, as explained above.

THE QUEEN—Cut a strip 4½" long by 1½" wide from a piece of white construction paper. Using your pencil, sketch the lines of the queen's crown on one end of the strip. (Note that we have used a zigzag shape for the king's crown and a semicircle design for the queen's.) When the crown is drawn to your satisfaction, use scissors to cut carefully along these lines. Crease the bottom of the figure to make the base, as described.

THE BISHOPS—Cut a strip 3½" long by 1½" wide from a piece of white construction paper. Using your pencil, sketch the lines for the bishop on one end of the strip. Here we have used a pointed arch to symbolize both the bishop's headpiece and the spire of a church. When the symbol is drawn to your satisfaction, use scissors to cut carefully along these lines. Crease the bottom of the figure to make the base, as described above. Repeat this procedure for the second bishop, using the first bishop as a pattern.

THE KNIGHTS—Cut a strip 3" long by 1½" wide from a piece of white construction paper. Using your pencil, sketch the lines of the horse's head on one end of the strip. Draw any type of horse you wish: show his ears, his nose, his tail, whatever design

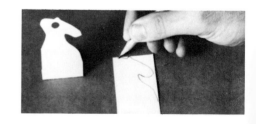

appeals to you. In our demonstration set we have given the horse an eye by using a paper-hole puncher. Crease the bottom of the figure to make the base, as described above. Repeat this procedure for second knight, using the first knight as a pattern.

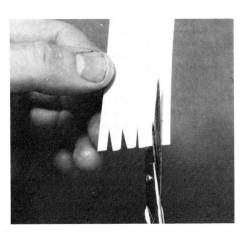

THE CASTLES—Cut a strip 3¼″ long by 1¼″ wide from a piece of white construction paper. Draw a straight line across the upper section of the castle, ½″ from the top. Lightly sketch eight evenly spaced lines perpendicular to this cross line, as shown. Cut along each of these short lines, and fold them back, as shown, to produce the illusion of a tower turret. In the demonstration set we have not erased the single line drawn on the upper section of the castle, as it gives proportion to the piece. Crease the bottom of the figure to make the base, as described above. Repeat this procedure for second castle, using the first castle as a pattern.

THE PAWNS—Cut a strip 2½″ long by ½″ wide from a piece of white construction paper. Punch a hole in the upper section of the pawn approximately ¼″ from the top, using a paper-hole puncher. Crease the bottom of the figure to make the base, as described above. Repeat this procedure for seven remaining pawns, using the first pawn as a pattern.

85

NOTE: When you have finished this set, thoroughly erase all pencil lines. The set is now ready. To make the black set, simply repeat the above directions. If you are going to use this set often, you might wish to add some weight to it so that the pieces will not fall over or tumble off the board. This can be done by taping or gluing a penny, paperclip, or any small flat object to the bottom of the bases.

You can use this set as is or decorate it with photographs, colors, cutouts, portraits, painted designs, etc. For decorating ideas consult the Wooden Chess Set. The silhouettes on this set can be cut to any designs you wish. Try, for example, making a set patterned on the New York (or any other city) skyline, making the World Trade Center king, the Empire State Building queen, the Chrysler Building bishops, etc. Or make silhouettes of famous people, particular animals, abstract shapes. Remember, you must always make drawings *first*. Never try to cut without a guideline.

THE ALUMINUM FOIL CHESS SET

If you're stranded on a desert island with a pile of foil gum-wrappers and a yearning to play chess, you're in luck: foil makes perfect chessmen. Though it is a common product, aluminum foil has many artistic uses. It can be cut, folded, and sculptured into endless shapes. Mistakes are easy to correct, either by making a few well-placed folds and creases or by scrapping the whole thing and starting again (foil is cheap and plentiful). You can make a highly attractive creation from foil, one which can be used once and tossed away or placed permanently in a spot of honor.

WHAT YOU WILL NEED TO MAKE THE SET

roll of aluminum foil (12″ width)
scissors

glue
ruler

HOW TO MAKE THE SET:

THE BASES—Instructions for making the bases will be given in the directions for making the individual chessmen.

THE KING—Pull approximately six inches of aluminum foil from the dispenser box. When tearing, be sure to rip neatly along the cutting edge. You should now have a piece of foil 6″ by 12″ in size. Make a number of 1″ folds across the width of the sheet, as shown, until you have a strip approximately 1″ wide by 12″ long. To make the base: make four or five 1″ overlapping folds at one end of the strip, as shown. Plant the piece firmly on the board with these folds serving as the base. The bases for all the other pieces will be made in the same way. Tear a piece of 3″ x 12″ foil from the roll and fold as above until you have a 1″ x 12″ strip. Wrap this strip around the upper section of the original strip, as shown. It is meant to represent the king's torso. Tear a 5″ x 12″ piece of foil from the roll, and roll rather than fold it into a long strip. Place a drop of glue on the center of this rolled strip and glue it onto the torso of the king. It thus becomes his arms. With scissors, cut the ends of the arms so they are in proportion to the rest of the body. For a finishing touch, roll a scrap of foil into a small scepter with a round top and glue it on one of the king's hands.

THE QUEEN—Follow the directions above, omitting the arms. Instead of arms the queen will have a crown. With scissors, snip seven or eight delicate cuts across the top of the queen's head so that a fan-shaped tiara emerges. You can make this headpiece as plain or as ornate as you wish. Extra pieces of foil, bits of colored paper, sequins, or painted ends can be added for extra effect.

THE BISHOPS—Tear a 6″ x 12″ piece of foil from the roll and cut it in half, making two 6″ x 6″ pieces. Fold one of these pieces several times, as we did above, until it measures approximately 6″ x 1″. Taper it at the top, as shown in the demonstration set, so that the bishop's head comes to a point. Fold the bottom part into a base, as described above. Repeat this procedure for second bishop, using the other 6″ x 6″ piece of foil.

THE KNIGHTS—Repeat the process described for the bishop, but do not taper the top of the strip. Instead, twist a small fold toward the upper section of the strip until it projects approximately ½″ from the body of the figure, as shown in the demonstration set. This represents the horse's head. Repeat this procedure for second knight.

THE CASTLES—Cut a 6″ x 6″ piece of foil, crease it three times, and fold it into a square, as shown. Repeat this procedure for second castle.

THE PAWNS—Fold a 3″ x 6″ piece of foil into a small standing piece as shown in the demonstration set. Repeat this procedure for seven remaining pawns.

> *NOTE:* Once the set is completed, remove all uneven edges at the bases or tops with scissors. To differentiate the black side from the white, spray one side with black paint and leave the other silver. Other ideas you may want to use:
>
> 1—Mold a nose and eyes for the king and queen by gluing small scraps of appropriately modeled foil onto their faces.
>
> 2—Give the horse a foil mane or tail.

3—Make the castle into a turret or a cylinder-shaped tower instead of a square one.

4—Glue a cross made from scraps of foil across the bishop's chest.

5—Make one side from aluminum foil and the other side from blue or red foil wrapping paper.

6—Add the following things to the figures to embellish them: ribbons, buttons, wire, paper scraps, sequins, or thread.

7—Use an appropriately sized piece of foil to make a board to go with this set. Foil is an impressionable substance. Simply spread a piece of it on the table, mark 64 even squares with a pencil or engraving instrument, and play.

EDIBLE CHESS SETS

First you buy the ingredients at the market. You take them home and make the chess pieces. You play the game. And finally, at the end of the match, the winner claims his prize—he gets to eat the set! This is the Edible Chess Set. The demonstration sets in this section are made of candy and cookies. You can as easily use bread molded into cubes and spheres, celery stalks and carrot tops, dried fruits and sugar cubes. Any foods which don't spoil too swiftly, which won't grease up the board, which in some way can be made to resemble the chessmen, and which can be made to stand up without toppling over are usable.

THE GUMDROP CHESS SET

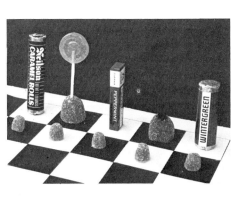

WHAT YOU WILL NEED TO MAKE THE SET

2—lollypops

6—large gumdrops

2—large rolls of caramels (or mints)

4—packages of chewing gum

1—package of twisted licorice sticks

4—packages of Lifesavers

16—small gumdrops

painted wooden bases

HOW TO MAKE THE SET:

THE BASES—Use regular wooden bases for the Gumdrop Chess Set. The instructions for these are given on page 24. If you wish to avoid using bases at all, simply make sure that the candies on one side are light (yellow, white, green, etc.) and the candies on the other side are dark (black, red, etc.).

THE KING—Push a medium-sized lollypop three-quarters of an inch into the center of a large gumdrop. Be sure that the lolly-pop doesn't slant and that it stands higher than the head of the queen. Place this onto a wooden base. Do *not* glue, especially if you intend to eat it in the end.

THE QUEEN—Stand a large roll of caramels (or mints) on end for the queen. Place this onto a wooden base. Do *not* glue, especially if you intend to eat it in the end. When shopping for this piece, make sure its base is large and flat enough to stand on its own without support.

THE BISHOPS—Place a package of chewing gum on the bishop's square, standing on end, as pictured. Do not glue to base. Repeat for second bishop.

THE KNIGHTS—Cut a three-inch strip of licorice and push it three-quarters of an inch into the center of a large gumdrop. After the licorice stick is embedded and balances in the base, bend the top so that it resembles the familiar shape of the knight. If the licorice stick keeps snapping back to its original shape, make a small cut at the underside of the bend. Do not glue to base. Repeat this procedure for second knight.

THE CASTLES—Place a package of Lifesavers on the castle's square, standing on end. Do not glue to base. Repeat for second castle.

THE PAWNS—Place a small gumdrop on a base. Do not glue to base. Repeat for seven remaining pawns.

> *NOTE:* The candies we have used here are only examples. Sets can be made from sourballs, bonbons, candy canes, chocolate bars and many other different kinds of candy.

THE COOKIE CHESS SET

WHAT YOU WILL NEED TO MAKE THE SET

two boxes of marshmallow cookies (one package of dark-colored cookies,
   one package of light)
one box of animal or toy cookies
kitchen knife

HOW TO MAKE THE SET:

THE BASES—Use the marshmallow cookies as bases—the dark-colored ones for the black side, the light-colored ones for the white.

THE PIECES—Empty out a box of toy or animal cookies. (In the demonstration sets, we use toy cookies.) Look through them for figures which recall particular qualities of the chess pieces. In the demonstration set, a soldier cookie is the king, a little girl cookie is the queen, sailboats are bishops (because they are pointed at the top like a bishop's hat), baby carriages are knights (because they have wheels and are thus mobile like the knight), and cottage-shaped cookies are castles (because they are buildings). For pawns we simply use the marshmallow cookies themselves without additions.

Once the toy cookies have been chosen, make a slit in the top of each marshmallow cookie base. A common kitchen knife is more than adequate for making the slits. Don't cut too deeply. If you do, you will cut into the bottom crust and the whole cookie will fall apart. Set the toy or animal cookies into these slits so that the cookies stand perfectly upright.

If the slit is made properly, not too wide or deep, the cookie should sit at the proper angle. Marshmallow is quite sticky and makes a surprisingly strong "glue." Once the toy or animal cookie is in place, it won't come unstuck very easily. The set is now ready for play. And of course, as with the Gumdrop Set, he who gains the checkmate also gains the feast.

THE NUT CHESS SET

The Nut Chess Set is another set in this series which you can eat when the contest is over. Unlike the others, however, the materials are not perishable and can remain chessmen as long as you wish, so the Nut Chess Set can be assembled either on a temporary or permanent basis. If you are going to use it permanently you can prolong the life of the nuts by waxing them with Butcher's Wax or by giving them an occasional burnishing with furniture polish. The selection of nuts made here is by no means exclusive: any walnut, almond or pistachio that looks good on the chess board will do.

WHAT YOU WILL NEED TO MAKE THE SET

2—large English walnuts   4—chestnuts
2—small English walnuts   16—hazelnuts (filberts)
4—pecans   painted wooden bases
4—Brazil nuts   glue (fast-drying)

HOW TO MAKE THE SET:

THE BASES—Use the regular wooden bases for the Nut Chess Set. The instructions for making these are given on page 24. If for some reason you wish to keep the nuts free of glue you can avoid the use of bases altogether—this set looks fine without a mounting. The only adjustment that you must make is to lay the bishop flat on his side rather than gluing him upright, as described in the directions below.

THE KING—Place a drop of glue on the flat underside of a large English walnut and mount it squarely onto a wooden base. Let dry.

THE QUEEN—Place a drop of glue on the flat underside of a small English walnut and mount it squarely onto a wooden base. Let dry.

THE BISHOPS—Stand a pecan on its flatest end. Place a drop of glue on this end and mount the nut squarely onto a wooden base. Hold it in position until the glue has set (a fast-drying glue will help). Let dry. Repeat for second bishop.

THE KNIGHTS—Place a drop of glue onto the flat underside of a Brazil nut and mount squarely onto a wooden base. Let dry. Most Brazil nuts are shaped in such a way that, if placed at the angle shown here, they give the general impression of a rearing horse (use your imagination), or at least a rearing animal. Repeat this procedure for second knight.

THE CASTLES—Place a drop of glue on the flat underside of a chestnut and mount it squarely onto a wooden base. Let dry. Repeat for second knight.

THE PAWNS—Place a drop of glue on the flat underside of a hazel (filbert) nut and mount it squarely onto a wooden base. Let dry. Repeat for seven remaining pawns.

> *NOTE:* When you have finished this set you can decorate it with paints or felt-tipped markers. You can also cover the pieces with glue and dip them (while still wet) into bowls of colored glitter: dark-colored glitter for the black side, light-colored for the white. These glitter-covered nuts, incidentally, make excellent Christmas tree ornaments as well as chessmen.

COIN CHESS SETS

The Coin Chess Set is one of several sets in this book which can either be put together on the spur of the moment when regular chess pieces are not available or assembled as a permanent piece. (If there's one lesson to be learned from this book, it's that lack of official chess pieces should never stop anyone from playing a game of chess.) In this set, the value of the coins and the value of the chess pieces are equivalent. The largest coin, the silver dollar, serves as king, the highest piece on the board; the second largest coin, the half dollar, serves as queen; and this sequence maintains itself all the way down the order of importance of the pieces. American coins of all denominations have been used to make this set. Foreign coins can also be used, or American and foreign coins can be mixed together to make an international set.

WHAT YOU WILL NEED TO MAKE THE SETS

glue
painted wooden bases
a collection of silver dollars, fifty cent pieces, quarters, dimes, nickels
and pennies. The amount of coins varies with the three sets here listed.

HOW TO MAKE THE SETS:

THE BASES—Standard wooden bases are used for these sets (see instructions on page 24). Or, in keeping with the theme of money, you may wish to use poker chips—black for the black side, red or white for the white side. If you plan to use any of these sets only once, it is not necessary to glue the coins together or to glue the pieces to the bases. If the set is to be permanent, glue the pieces to the bases. Since it is illegal to deface American currency, use a dissolvable glue such as rubber cement on the coins.

THE $4.96 CHESS SET

The $4.96 Chess Set is the simplest of the three coin chess sets.

WHAT YOU WILL NEED TO MAKE THE SET

2—*silver dollars*

2—*fifty cent pieces*

4—*dimes*

8—*nickels*

4—*quarters*

16—*pennies*

painted wooden bases

glue (optional)

THE KING—Place a silver dollar onto a wooden base.

THE QUEEN—Place a fifty cent piece onto a wooden base.

THE BISHOPS—Place a dime onto a wooden base. Repeat for second bishop.

THE KNIGHTS—Place two nickels onto a wooden base. Repeat for second knight.

THE CASTLES—Place a quarter onto a wooden base. Repeat for second castle.

THE PAWNS—Place a penny onto a wooden base. Repeat for seven remaining pawns.

THE $10.36 CHESS SET

This set requires more coins. Again, if you wish to make the set permanent, simply glue the coins to each other and to their bases, as required.

WHAT YOU WILL NEED TO MAKE THE SET

2—*silver dollars*
4—*fifty cent pieces*
16—*quarters*
16—*pennies*

12—*nickels*
16—*dimes*
painted wooden bases
glue (optional)

THE KING—Stack on a wooden base in the following order: a silver dollar, a fifty cent piece, two quarters, a nickel, and a dime.

THE QUEEN—Stack the following coins in order onto a base: a fifty cent piece, two quarters, a nickel, and a dime.

THE BISHOPS—Stack three dimes onto a base, making sure they are perfectly centered. Repeat for second bishop.

THE KNIGHTS—Stack three nickels onto a base, making sure they are perfectly centered. Repeat for second knight.

THE CASTLES—Stack two quarters onto a base, making sure they are perfectly centered. Repeat for second castle.

THE PAWNS—Place one penny onto a base. Repeat for seven remaining pawns.

THE $40.48 CHESS SET

This set is for those who have plenty of change in their pockets. Although a lot of coins are used in building it, the total is only $20.24 for one side—and it's not as if you are spending it anyway. The coins for this set can be purchased in coin-rolls from any bank. Again, if you want to make the set permanent, simply glue the coins to each other and to their bases, as required.

WHAT YOU WILL NEED TO MAKE THE SET

6—silver dollars	32—nickels
4—fifty cent pieces	48—pennies
64—quarters	painted wooden bases
144—dimes	glue

THE KING—Place a silver dollar onto a base. Mount a fifty cent piece on the silver dollar. Stack twelve quarters onto the fifty cent piece and crown the pile with another silver dollar. Stack three quarters, three dimes, a nickel and another quarter, in that order, on top of the second silver dollar.

THE QUEEN—Onto a base. Stack a silver dollar and eleven quarters. Cap these with a fifty cent piece. Stack one quarter, one nickel, and three dimes, in that order, on top of the fifty cent piece.

THE BISHOPS—Stack fifteen dimes onto a base, making sure the pile is centered. Repeat for second bishop.

THE KNIGHTS—Place a nickel onto a base. On top of the nickel, stack a dime, a nickel, then a dime, then another nickel, and so on, until you have seven nickels with six dimes staggered between them. Repeat for second knight.

THE CASTLES—Place a quarter onto a base. Stack twelve dimes onto the quarter, and cap it with a second quarter.

THE PAWNS—Stack three pennies onto a base, making sure the pile is centered. Repeat for seven remaining pawns.

MISCELLANEOUS CHESS SETS

THE CORNSTARCH FIGURE CHESS SET

Cornstarch is a staple in the kitchen that can be used for making creative objects. (Perhaps you have seen cornstarch Christmas tree ornaments. The process used to make them is the same one we will use here.) Mix a dough, cut it into shapes, bake it, paint the pieces, and mount them on bases. That is all there is to it. You will then have a colorful chess set which looks as if it were modeled out of clay, but which takes half the time and a tenth of the equipment required to make ceramic figurines.

WHAT YOU WILL NEED TO MAKE THE SET

2—cups cornstarch
4—cups baking soda
   (2 pounds)
2½—cups water
saucepan and mixing
   spoon
flat plate
damp cloth or paper
   towel
waxed paper
flour
rolling pin
cookie cutters (Since
   you are making a
   chess set, you will
   need a different cut-
   ter for each piece. In
   this set we use a Santa
Claus cutter for the
king, a club-shaped
cutter for the queen,
a cross for the bishop,
a deer for the knight,
a tree for the castle,
small human figures
for pawns, and a
round cutter 1½" in
diameter for the
base.
spatula
fine sandpaper
paint or other coloring
brushes
varnish or clear plastic
   spray
fast-drying glue

HOW TO MAKE THE SET:

STEP ONE—Mix the cornstarch, baking soda, and water in a saucepan, using the proportions listed in the materials section above. Heat, stirring constantly, until the mixture comes to a low boil. Continue stirring until the dough reaches a mashed-potato-like consistency.

STEP TWO—Remove the dough from the saucepan, place on a plate and cover with a damp cloth or paper towel. Store in the refrigerator for an hour.

STEP THREE—Remove dough and knead it for 4 to 5 minutes until it becomes as thick and consistent as a bread dough.

STEP FOUR—Spread a piece of waxed paper out on a flat surface. Sprinkle some flour over the working area to prevent the dough from sticking to the waxed paper. Use a rolling pin to roll the dough flat onto the waxed paper until it reaches a consistent thickness of ¼″.

STEP FIVE—When the dough is flat, use your cookie cutters to cut out the pieces. Remember: for *each side* the king and queen require one figure apiece, the bishop, knight, and castle two identical pieces, and the pawns eight identical pieces; sixteen round (or square if you prefer) bases should also be cut for each side. If you have enough dough left over, cut duplicates in case some of the pieces come out damaged or imperfect after baking. Be careful with the dough while cutting the chessmen. It crumbles easily. Also, when cutting the pieces you may wish to give them added decoration. You can, for instance, make holes in the pieces with paper clips or toothpicks, roll small balls of dough and press them firmly onto the ornaments, or draw patterns on the surface of the pieces.

STEP SIX—Place the ornaments on a cookie sheet. Preheat the oven to 350°, turn it off, and put the cookie sheet into the oven. When the top surface is baked hard (approximately 40 minutes), turn the pieces over with a spatula, being careful not to damage them. The pieces have a tendency to harden on the outside and stay uncooked on the inside, so be careful to keep them in the oven for an adequate length of time. Keep a few test pieces on the sheet; when they are hard on both sides, they are done.

STEP SEVEN—When pieces are properly baked, remove from oven and let cool. Use some fine sandpaper to clean off the rough surfaces.

STEP EIGHT—Decorate the chessmen and bases in whatever way you wish—with poster paints, plastic-base enamel, nail polish, water colors, magic markers. The cornstarch surface will accept practically any kind of coloring. Be sure, however, that you make one set predominantly dark and the other predominantly light. (You may wish instead to paint the bases of one side black and the bases of the other white—this leaves you more freedom in choosing the colors for the chessmen.) When you have painted the pieces, give each a coat of varnish, or spray with clear plastic spray.

STEP NINE—Squeeze a few drops of glue onto the bottom of a chessman. Mount it onto a base, and prop it against a supportive surface while it dries. Repeat this procedure for each of the pieces, being sure they are mounted in the center of the bases. Let dry. Remove any excess glue that may have accumulated on the bases. The set is now complete.

THE PLASTIC CUBE CHESS SET

If you have admired the sleek acrylic chess sets in mail-order catalogs and gift shops, you will be pleased to learn that what appears to be a complicated and expensive item is really quite simple to make and inexpensive. Materials for this set can be purchased from plastic and glass suppliers located in all big cities and in most large towns. They can also be ordered by mail from wholesalers. One firm that sells a wide variety of plastics through a mail-order catalog is *Mail Order Plastics, 56 Lispenard Street, New York, N.Y. 10013*. Looking through their catalog you will get a good idea of the costs in assembling an acrylic cube set.

Mail Order Plastics, like most plastic dealers, also sells acrylic balls, domes, tubing, boxes, etc., any of which can be used to build chess sets.

WHAT YOU WILL NEED TO MAKE THE SET

20—1″ acrylic cubes	32—clear 2″ acrylic discs
16—⅝″ acrylic cubes	clear plastic cement
58—½″ acrylic cubes	black paint and brush

HOW TO MAKE THE SET:

THE BASES—The pieces in the Plastic Cube Chess Set stand on 2" acrylic discs. Prepare these discs by painting one side of them black and using the painted side as the *bottom* of the base, the side that faces the board. (The discs for the white side should be left unpainted.) The painted surfaces of the discs will receive a certain amount of scuffing during play, so it is advisable to coat them with a clear vinyl spray which will help resist all rubbing and protect the chessboard. The most efficient way to apply plastic cement is with a small brush (sometimes these come with the glue can). Dip the brush lightly into the container of cement and with even strokes apply it to the surface of the cube. When using plastic cement, remember that it dries very fast, almost on contact. It is thus important that the cubes be joined *immediately* after the cement is applied, and that the joining be precise. If the cubes are cemented together in a sloppy manner, there will be little time to correct them before they are frozen in place. Once bonded, plastic parts are not easy to separate.

NOTE: All cements and cleaners can be purchased from suppliers. Plastic cement stains plastic surfaces. When applying it, be careful not to smudge it on the unglued surfaces of the cubes. If this does happen, plastic cleaner can be used to remove the blemishes if they are not too severe.

THE KING—Cement three 1″ acrylic cubes one on top of the other like building blocks so that the edges of all three are perfectly even. Cement a ⅝″ cube to the center of one end of the three-cube assembly. Cement a ½″ cube to the center of the ⅝″ cube. Let dry. You should now have a five-cube-high chess piece. Mount onto the base, making sure the figure is placed directly in the center of the disc.

THE QUEEN—Cement three 1″ acrylic cubes one on top of the other, so that the edges of all three are perfectly even. Cement a ⅝″ cube to the center of one end of the three-cube assembly. Let dry. Mount this four-cube assembly figure onto the base, making sure it is placed directly in the center of the disc.

THE BISHOPS—On any flat surface, arrange five ½″ acrylic cubes into the shape of a cross, as shown. Do not apply any cement until you are certain how the cubes should be arranged and joined. Once the cross is made, mount it onto a ⅝″ acrylic cube, as shown. Let dry. Mount the whole whole piece onto the base, making sure the figure is placed directly onto the center of the disc. Repeat this procedure for second bishop.

THE KNIGHTS—Cement a ⅝″ acrylic cube directly onto the center of a 1″ cube. Let dry. Apply cement to approximately *half* of one surface of a ½″ cube. Place the cemented half onto the top of the ⅝″ cube, as shown, so that it overlaps, representing the horse's head. The glue is strong and will hold the protruding piece in this position without difficulty. Let dry. Mount onto the base, making sure the figure is placed directly onto the center of the disc. Repeat this procedure for second knight.

THE CASTLES—Cement a ⅝″ acrylic cube directly onto the center of a 1″ cube. Let dry. Mount this figure onto the center of a disc base using the ⅝″ (smaller) cube as bottom support, as shown in the demonstration set. Repeat this procedure for second castle.

THE PAWNS—Cement two ½″ acrylic cubes together so that the edges are evenly aligned. Let dry. Mount this figure onto a base, being sure it is placed directly onto the center of the disc. Repeat this procedure for seven remaining pawns.

> *NOTE:* When the set is completed it can be shined with anti-static cleaner, available from any supplier.

The plastic parts sold at the supplier's should give you many more ideas for chess sets. Sets can be made from plastic balls, plastic tubing, different-colored plastic boxes, and so forth, plus combinations of these. Screws, bolts, gears, plastic beads, styrofoam pieces, rocks, jewelry—any number of objects can be added to the plastic parts once they are assembled. Here, for example, we have crowned the queen with a lead weight sinker in one picture and a ball bearing in another. The cubes might be painted on one side with silver paint to give a mirror-like effect; or actual small, round mirrors can be used as bases. Study the catalogs and the display at the supplier's for other ideas.

THE CORK AND BOTTLE CAP CHESS SET

The corks used in this set have come from a variety of bottles. The majority were taken from wine, vermouth, brandy, and liquor bottles, though some came from test tubes and medicine jars. Corks can be purchased directly from the manufacturer, from pharmacies, or from hardware stores. They can also be rescued from old bottles bound for disposal. Any tavern will no doubt have a large number to give away. In your hunt for corks do not expect to find many perfect specimens, especially among those which have already been removed from the bottle, for the corkscrew invariably leaves its mark. As in the other sets in this book, it is not necessary to match exactly the corks we use in the demonstration set. You need only understand the concept of the set and

then make one of your own design. We will thus give the dimensions of each cork in the materials list, but this is for general information rather than specific direction.

WHAT YOU WILL NEED TO MAKE THE SET

1—2" *screw-on plastic bottle cap*   (*from Asti-Gancia bottle*)
1—1½" *bottle cork with metal or plastic top*   (*from WT&S bottle*)
1—¾" *test-tube cork*
1—2" *screw-on plastic bottle cap*   (*no brand name on cap*)
1—1" *bottle cork with plastic or metal top*   (*from WT&S bottle*)
1—¾" *test-tube cork*
2—1½" *bottle corks with metal or plastic tops*
4—2" *screw-on plastic bottle caps*
6—*straight pins*
12—¾" *test-tube corks*
6—1" *bottle corks with plastic or metal tops*
4—1½" *wine bottle corks*
4—2" *bottle corks with rounded plastic tops*
16—½" *bottle corks with plastic or metal tops*
painted wooden bases
fine sandpaper
glue

HOW TO MAKE THE SET:

THE BASES—Use regular wooden bases for the Cork Chess Set. The instructions for these are given on page **24**. Note that you can remedy a cork which will not stand up on the base correctly, by gently sanding the trouble spot with a piece of fine sandpaper until it is smooth. A cork surface will sand nicely as long as you make certain to use *fine* sandpaper for the job.

THE KING—Stand a 1½″ bottle cork with metal or plastic cap top-downward, as shown. Place a few drops of glue onto the protruding cork end. Place a 2″ screw-on plastic bottle cap onto the glued surface cap-downward, and let dry. Cap the whole thing off by gluing a ¾″ test-tube cork onto the top of the plastic bottle cap and let dry. Mount onto base. As an extra ornament we have placed a straight pin into the test-tube cork, protruding a half-inch from the crown.

THE QUEEN—Stand a 2″ screw-on plastic cap cap-downward, as shown. Place a few drops of glue around the protruding rim. Place a 1″ bottle cork with plastic or metal top onto the glued rim, cap-downward. Let dry. To finish the piece, glue a ¾″ test-tube cork onto the protruding cork end of the 1″ bottle cork. Let dry. Mount onto base.

THE BISHOPS—Glue a ¾″ test-tube cork onto the top of a 1½″ wine bottle cork. Let dry. Mount onto base. Repeat this procedure for second bishop.

THE KNIGHTS—Stand a 1″ bottle cork with plastic or metal cap top-downward. Place a few drops of glue onto the protruding cork end. Place another 1″ cork, also cap-downward, on the center of this glued surface. Let dry. With a straight pin, attach a ¾″ test-tube cork to the top cork, as shown.

THE CASTLES—Stand a 2″ bottle cork with a rounded plastic cap top-downwards, as shown. Mount onto a base. Repeat this procedure for second castle.

THE PAWNS—Stand a ½″ bottle cork with plastic or metal cap top-downward, as shown. Mount onto a base. Repeat this procedure for seven remaining pawns.

> *NOTE:* The decoration of this set can be carried one step further by painting, coloring, or drawing faces, designs, etc. directly onto the pieces. Both water- and oil-based paints go smoothly onto a cork surface, as do the colors from felt-tipped pens.

THE THREAD SPOOL CHESS SET

Here is a colorful set which can be fashioned from the contents of a sewing basket. Spools of different color thread, five-color thread-rolls, buttons and thimbles are the materials you will need. They are available at any dime or notions store. We have used a variety of different-colored spools because the colorful effect is appealing to the eye. If you prefer, you can make the black side completely out of dark-colored thread spools and the white side out of light. This would make the wooden bases unnecessary, should you care to leave them out. The size of each spool, incidentally, is not given on the spool's label, so when you shop for the materials it is advisable to bring along a small ruler or tape measure. Either styrofoam or wooden thread spools can be used for this set.

WHAT YOU WILL NEED TO MAKE THE SET

8—1″ x 1″ spools
2—2″ x 1½″ spools
12—1″ x ¾″ spools
2—thimbles
4—½″ buttons
6—1½″ x 1¼″ spools

4—five-color 2″ thread rolls
26—⅝″ x ⅝″ spools
painted wooden bases
glue

HOW TO MAKE THE SET:

THE BASES—Use regular wooden bases for the Thread Spool Chess Set. The instructions for these are given on page 24.

THE KING—Center and glue a 1" x 1" spool on top of a 2" x 1½" spool. Center and glue a 1" x ¾" spool on top of this construction. You now have a three-step pyramid of spools. Crown the whole piece with a thimble. Glue a button onto the side center of the top spool, as shown. Let dry. Mount onto a wooden base.

THE QUEEN—Center and glue a 1" x 1" spool to the top of a 1½" x 1¼" spool. Center and glue a 1" x ¾" spool on top of this construction. You now have a three-step pyramid slightly shorter than the three spools of the king. Crown the piece with a ⅝" x ⅝" spool. Glue a button to the center of the top spool, as shown. Let dry. Mount onto a wooden base.

THE BISHOPS—Squeeze a little glue onto one rim of a five-colored thread roll. Mount a 1" x ¾" spool onto that rim. Let dry. Mount onto a wooden base. Repeat this procedure for the second bishop.

133

THE KNIGHTS—Center and glue a 1″ x 1″ spool onto a ⅝″ x ⅝″ spool. Glue another ⅝″ x ⅝″ spool onto the middle of the 1″ x 1″ spool, as shown. Let dry. Mount onto a wooden base. Repeat this procedure for second knight.

THE CASTLES—Center and glue a 1½″ x 1¼″ spool onto a 1″ x ¾″ spool. Let dry. Mount onto a wooden base. Repeat this procedure for second castle.

THE PAWNS—Mount a ⅝″ x ⅝″ spool onto a wooden base, making sure the spool is directly centered. Let dry. Repeat this procedure for seven remaining pawns.

> *NOTE:* The spools in this set can be arranged in many other combinations. Experiment with them. Try putting buttons all over each piece, or stripping the thread off some spools and painting them with colors and designs.

THE PILL AND CAPSULE CHESS SET

The Pill and Capsule Chess Set makes a good gift for a doctor, nurse, vitamin lover, pharmacist, etc. It calls for materials which can easily be found and are readily assembled. The pills we use are vitamins. Almost everyone will have vitamin tablets and capsules in his own medicine chest which approximate those given in the materials list. It's not necessary to buy new pills in order to make this set.

WHAT YOU WILL NEED TO MAKE THE SET

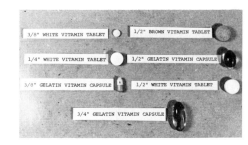

6—½" white vitamin tablets

2—½" gelatin vitamin capsules

2—¾" gelatin vitamin capsules

18—½" brown or white vitamin tablets

8—⅜" white vitamin tablets

4—⅜" gelatin vitamin capsules

16—¼" white vitamin tablets

48—bottle caps

black (or red) and white paint with brushes

glue—Duco cement or other fast-drying glue

razor or sharp knife

fine sandpaper

HOW TO MAKE THE SET:

THE BASES—Bottle caps are used as bases for this set. Normal-sized wooden or tile bases are too large (the tiny pills would be greatly out of proportion if mounted on large bases) and the toothed edges of the bottle caps complement the shape of the pills themselves. Bottle caps can be purchased from hardware stores, wine makers' supply catalogs, or collected from used bottles. Glue thirty-two bottle caps base-to-base, as shown, so that the edges are neatly aligned. These sixteen double bases will be used as mounts for the major pieces, while sixteen single, unjoined caps will be used to hold the pawns. Use black or red paint to paint the tops of the caps, being careful to maintain an even circle all around. (We have used red here—it is a pleasant change from black and contrasts nicely with the colors of the capsules.) Do the same for the white caps. The bases are now ready.

THE KING—Place a drop of glue onto a ½″ white vitamin tablet and mount it onto a double base. Let dry. Place another small drop of glue on top of this tablet and mount a second ½″ white vitamin pill on the first one, making sure that both pills are centered on the base. Let dry. Place a small amount of glue onto one end of a 1″ gelatin vitamin capsule and set it vertically atop the second pill, making sure the capsule stands straight. Let dry.

THE QUEEN—Place a drop of glue onto a ½″ white vitamin tablet and mount it onto a double base. Let dry. Place a small amount of glue onto one end of a ¾″ gelatin capsule and set it vertically atop the tablet, making sure the capsule stands straight. Let dry.

THE BISHOPS—Place a drop of glue onto a brown or white ½″ vitamin tablet and mount it onto a double base. Let dry. Place a small drop of glue on top of this tablet and mount a ⅜″ white vitamin tablet on it, making sure that both pills are centered on the base. Let dry. Place a small amount of glue onto one end of a ⅜″ gelatin capsule and set it vertically atop the second pill, making sure the capsule stands straight. Let dry. Repeat this procedure for second bishop.

THE KNIGHTS—Place a drop of glue onto a ½″ brown or white vitamin tablet and mount it onto a double base. Let dry.

Choose another ½″ vitamin tablet, preferably one with a crease in it for easy division, and cut it neatly in two with a razor or sharp knife. If the cut surface is at all rough, a couple of gentle strokes with fine sandpaper will smooth it. Place a drop of glue onto one half of the cut pill and mount it onto the ½″ vitamin tablet, curved side up. Let dry. Repeat this procedure for second knight.

THE CASTLES—Place a drop of glue onto a ½″ brown or white vitamin tablet and mount it onto a double base. Let dry. Place a small drop of glue on top of this tablet and mount another ½″ vitamin tablet on it. Let dry. Place a drop of glue onto the second tablet and mount a ⅜″ white vitamin tablet on it, making sure that all three pills are centered in relation to each other and to their base. Let dry. Repeat this procedure for second castle.

THE PAWNS—Place a drop of glue onto a ¼″ white vitamin tablet and mount it onto a single-cap base, making sure the pill is placed in the exact center of the base. Let dry. Repeat for seven remaining pawns.

SOME IMPROVISED CHESS SETS

THE FIGURINE CHESS SET

Figurines can be bought very inexpensively in any stationery, dime, gift, or toy store. You can also put together an interesting and personal set using figurines you find around the house. Although we don't recommend drafting heirlooms in the service of chess, some readily adaptable objects are: lead, wooden or plastic soldiers, pottery figures, porcelain miniatures, small wood carvings, tiny dolls (or big ones, if you have a big board), toy cars, toy planes, toy trucks, toy buses, ivory carvings, blown glass statuary, plaster castings, electric train miniatures, marble busts, cast-iron knickknacks, figures made of china and storeware, and soap carvings. The following three sets are improvised from toy soldiers and figurines. The first is made from plastic soldiers, the second from miniature rubber toy animals and the third from plaster cast models from India.

THE KITCHEN CHESS SET

Every kitchen contains different possibilities for assembling a chess set. The wonderful shapes, forms and designs of kitchen objects—everything from cutlery to ketchup bottles—can all be adapted to the chess board. Examine the contents of your kitchen cupboards. Look at the cans, the bottles, the salt and pepper shakers, and consider how they might be combined. The results should be interesting. In the first set shown here we have used groceries and foodstuffs; in the second we have used kitchen implements. Household sets do not stop in the kitchen. You can try making a bathroom chess set (check the medicine cabinet; it is a goldmine), a living room chess set, a basement chess set, and so on. Every room in the house has *something* to contribute.

THE ROCKS AND STONES CHESS SET

Perhaps you are camping, with no access to household objects, and you still want to make a chess set. You can clear a small piece of ground to make a board. Stones or sticks can serve to outline the border and squares, or you can simply scratch a board in the dirt or sand. Spend a few minutes searching for stones, remembering the various sizes of the chess pieces themselves: the two biggest stones should be king and queen; long, thin stones should serve as bishops; jagged eccentric stones as knights; round, heavy stones as castles; and pebbles as the pawns. Use darker stones for the black pieces (they can also be stained dark with shoe polish, soot, etc.), light stones for white. The set and board shown here were assembled in just this manner.

ANYTHING CAN BE MADE INTO A CHESS SET

By reading this book it should now be clear that practically anything can be made into a chess set. The purpose of this book has been not only to show how the sets are made, but to stimulate your thinking along similar lines, to help you see shapes for the chessboard in the everyday objects of your environment. Below are a few more suggestions for materials which can be transformed into chess sets.

1) *Potted Plants*—Use small pots with, say, herbs in them for the pawns. Use larger plants for the major pieces, and plants with flowers for the king and queen.
2) *Candles*—Here's a nighttime spectacle. Find a relatively wind-free location out-of-doors, mark the dimensions of a large chessboard on a lawn or any flat space (you can draw it with chalk on blacktop if no lawn is available), and use candles of

different heights as pieces. (If you have interesting candle-holders, better yet; a big candelabrum would make a beautiful king.) Choose a summer night and a spot removed from all fire hazards. Set the pieces up, light them, and play the game. The light from the candles will illuminate the entire board.

3) *Shells*—Shells, either those found on the beach or those bought at a store, can be made into exotic and unusual chessmen. They look especially beautiful if mounted on transparent plastic cubes (see the Plastic Cube Chess Set, page 120, for more information).

4) *Pens, Pencils, Crayons*—A quill pen makes the king, a smaller quill the queen. Pencils are bishops, marking crayons are knights, magic markers are castles, bits of crayons are pawns. If you want to mount them on bases try using soap erasers.

5) *Marbles*—Marbles can be joined and mounted in the same way as the ball bearings in the Ball Bearing Chess Set (page 26).

6) *Wooden Branches*—Interesting branches are used for the major pieces, twigs for the pawns—all are glued onto wooden bases. (Sometimes checkers can be used in place of the standard wooden bases—they come already colored in black and red.)

7) *Assorted Hardware*—Let yourself loose in a hardware store and combine the springs, hooks, nozzles, and switches you see on the rack into chess sets. You can also find interesting miscellaneous items in army surplus stores, drugstores, junk and antique stores, wrecking and salvage yards, hobby shops, art supply stores, toy shops, music shops and many other places.

8) *Picture Chess Set*—Cut out pictures and mount them on wooden dowels, blocks, cardboard mountings, fiberboard backings, plastic frames, etc. Pick a set of pictures belonging to the same time, place, story, or institution: World War I generals, mythological personalities, great statues, famous landmarks, political figures, entertainers, people in the news. You might make different teams for your sets. You might have a political team taking on a group of cartoon characters from the Sunday comic strips. Any combination of opponents can be created: old motion picture stars compete with the New York Mets; wild African animals challenge automobiles; cowboys play Indians . . . or astronauts . . . or Greek gods. Anyone can play anyone. The possibilities are unlimited. You can make a family album set. Take old pictures of your family

and friends. Make father the king, mother the queen, and brothers, sisters, sons, and daughters the rest of the pieces, with pets or babies as the pawns. The same set can be made by using pictures of business associates, friends, even enemies if you like. Any political group on a local, state, or international level can provide interesting material.

MAKE YOUR OWN BOARD

Try making your own board. There are sixty-four squares on a chessboard, arranged in eight rows of eight squares each. Each square should measure from one to two inches square.

	1	2	3	4	5	6	7	8
	2							
	3							
1″–2″	4							
	5							
	6							
	7							
	8							

Using a ruler as a guide, mark the lines in pen, pencil, or brush, and color in the black squares with paint or a magic marker.

Boards can be sketched on blackboards and erased when the game is finished. They can be drawn on the sidewalk in chalk. They can be assembled from the square bathroom tiles we used as bases in the Screw Chess Set and the Plumbing Parts Chess Set. They can be made by pasting down dark and light squares of paper, matchcovers, dried leaves cut into squares, plastic boxes.

Here are more things that can be made into chess sets:

bottle caps
boxes of all kinds
bricks (paint them)
cardboard
carved soap
chain links
clock parts
coat hangers
copper tubing
cutout dolls
darts
dolls
doorknobs
driftwood
drinking glasses
fabric
film cassettes
fishing line sinkers
flashbulbs

flashlights
hinges
incense sticks
jewelry
keys
knives and spoons
knobs
lamps
lamp crystals
lamp tops
light bulbs
locks
matchsticks
medallions
milk cartons
mirrors
nuts and bolts
paintbrushes
paper clips

paperweights
perfume bottles
pipes
pipe cleaners
pushpins
putty, molded
rings
salt and pepper shakers
flags (miniatures)
soap erasers
spice jars
staircase spindles
stuffed socks and beans
styrofoam
test tubes
tinker toys
toothpicks
tops
vases